BASIC MATERIALS

Note: A list of materials needed for beginners is located on page 5.

Crochet requires only a few essentials, and the next few pages will show what you need to get started. Different types of hooks and yarns will be explained, and a variety of crocheting accessories will be covered.

CROCHET HOOKS

There are several types of crochet hooks. Let's first take a look at the structure of a crochet hook, and then go on to see the different kinds and sizes that are available.

ANATOMY OF A CROCHET HOOK

A crochet hook can be divided into five different sections, with each section having its own purpose *(Fig. 1)*.

Fig. 1

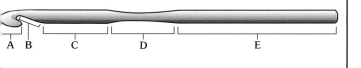

- Hook - end used to catch yarn or thread and pull it through other loops.

- Throat - shaped section that guides yarn or thread up onto working area.

- Working area - section where stitches are worked.

- Finger hold - indented section for gripping hook with your thumb and index or third finger.

- Handle - balancing end that rests under remaining fingers or lays over hand.

ALUMINUM, PLASTIC, AND WOOD HOOKS

These types of crochet hooks are used with all types of yarns and cotton fabrics. Aluminum is currently the most popular material used for manufacturing crochet hooks.

The size of a hook is determined by the diameter of its working area. In addition to being measured in millimeters *(abbreviated mm)*, each size is also assigned a letter. Lettered hooks range from size B (2.25 mm), the smallest, to size Q (15.00 mm), the largest *(Fig. 2)*.

The **more advanced** the letter, the **larger** the hook.

Fig. 2

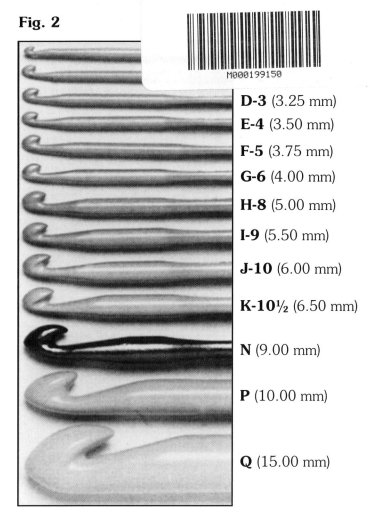

D-3 (3.25 mm)
E-4 (3.50 mm)
F-5 (3.75 mm)
G-6 (4.00 mm)
H-8 (5.00 mm)
I-9 (5.50 mm)
J-10 (6.00 mm)
K-10½ (6.50 mm)
N (9.00 mm)
P (10.00 mm)
Q (15.00 mm)

STEEL HOOKS

Steel crochet hooks are primarily used when working with threads and finer yarns.

The diameters of steel hooks are also measured in millimeters, but each size is assigned a number instead of a letter. Steel hooks range from size 00 (3.50 mm), the largest, to size 14 (0.75 mm), the smallest *(Fig. 3)*.

The **larger** the number, the **smaller** the hook.

Fig. 3

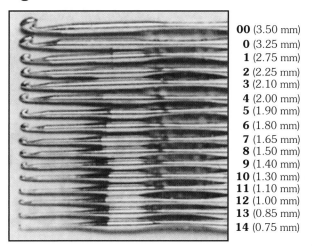

00 (3.50 mm)
0 (3.25 mm)
1 (2.75 mm)
2 (2.25 mm)
3 (2.10 mm)
4 (2.00 mm)
5 (1.90 mm)
6 (1.80 mm)
7 (1.65 mm)
8 (1.50 mm)
9 (1.40 mm)
10 (1.30 mm)
11 (1.10 mm)
12 (1.00 mm)
13 (0.85 mm)
14 (0.75 mm)

YARNS AND THREADS

An amazing array of yarn and thread is available to the crocheter. Yarns and threads are usually purchased in balls or skeins. A skein differs from a ball in that the yarn or thread is pulled out from its center to keep it from unrolling.

YARNS

Yarn ranges from thick bulky yarn to very fine baby yarn. All yarn is classified by weight which is determined by the thickness of the strand. Worsted weight yarn is the most popular and readily available. **Fig. 4** shows a sample of the most commonly used yarn weights.

Fig. 4

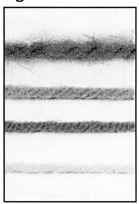

Bulky weight
(heavy sweaters, pot holders, afghans)

Worsted weight
(sweaters, afghans, toys)

Sport weight
(baby clothes, sweaters, afghans)

Baby weight
(baby clothes)

Yarn is made from many materials. Natural fibers include cotton, wool, silk, mohair, and alpaca. Synthetic fibers are man-made and include acrylics, polyester, and viscose. You will often find yarn blended with several different types of fibers.

Yarn consists of individual strands twisted together called "plies." The number of plies indicates the number of strands twisted together and has nothing to do with the weight of the yarn.

When selecting yarn, try to choose the fiber and weight best suited for your project.

DYE LOTS

Yarn is dyed in large batches. Each batch is referred to a a "dye lot" and is assigned a number which will be listed on the yarn label *(Fig. 5)*. The color will vary slightly in shade from one dye lot to another. This color variance may be noticeable if skeins of yarn from different dye lo are used together in your project.

So, when purchasing more than one skein of yarn for a particular color in your project, be sure to select skeins c yarn labeled with **identical** dye lot numbers.

READING A YARN LABEL

Yarn labels provide you with important information that is helpful in selecting the type of yarn needed and the number of skeins necessary for your project. Labels from different yarn companies may vary, so be sure to read them carefully. **Fig. 5** illustrates a sample yarn label.

1. Color number and name

2. Dye lot number

3. Yarn brand name

4. Ply and weight

5. Type of yarn - wool, cotton, etc.

6. Grams or ounces per ball or skein

7. Yards per ball or skein

8. Suggested knitting or crochet gauge

9. Washing instructions (sometimes this will be listed on the inside of the label)

Fig. 5

SUBSTITUTING YARNS

Once you know the weight of the yarn specified for a particular pattern, any brand of the **same** weight may be used for that pattern.

You may wish to purchase a single skein first and crochet a gauge swatch *(see Gauge, page 22)*. Compare your gauge to the gauge specified in the pattern and make sure it matches. Then compare the way the new yarn looks to the photographed item to be sure that you'll be satisfied with the finished results.

The number of skeins to buy depends on the yardage. Compare labels and ask the shop owner if you need assistance. Ounces and grams can vary from one brand of the same weight yarn to another, but the yardage required to make an item will always remain the same.

THREADS

The most common type of crochet thread is made from cotton. There are many sizes (also referred to as weights) of crochet cotton. Thread sizes range from a thick size 3 to a thin, delicate size 150. The **higher** the size number, the **thinner** the thread. The most popular thread size is bedspread weight cotton, size 10. **Fig. 6** shows a few of the most commonly used cotton crochet threads.

Fig. 6

	Cotton crochet thread, size 5
	Cotton crochet thread, size 8
	Bedspread weight cotton crochet thread, size 10
	Cotton crochet thread, size 20
	Cotton crochet thread, size 30

The type of thread you choose for a project will depend on the item you are making and the size recommended in the instructions. Sizes 5 and 8 are generally used for vests and other garments. Smaller sizes are preferred for doilies, baby items, tablecloths, snowflakes, and edgings.

TIPS FOR PURCHASING YARN AND THREAD

. Always purchase the same **weight** yarn or thread as specified in your project instructions.

. It is best to refer to the yardage to determine how many skeins to purchase, since the number of yards per ounce may vary from one brand to another.

. For each color in your project, purchase skeins in the same dye lot at one time, or you may risk being unable to find the same dye lot again.

. If you are unsure if you will have enough yarn or thread, buy an extra skein. Some stores will allow you to return unused skeins. Ask your local yarn shop about their return policy.

ADDITIONAL ACCESSORIES

There are many different types of accessories available to assist you with your projects. **Fig. 7** shows a few of the items you may want to purchase.

Fig. 7

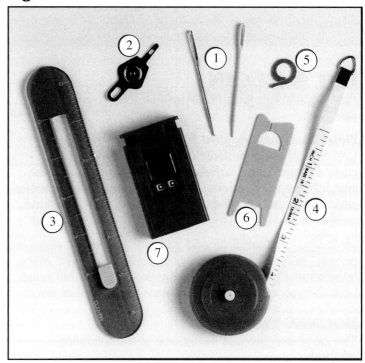

1. Yarn or tapestry needles - used for weaving in yarn ends, whipstitching crocheted pieces together, sewing seams, or attaching finishing touches. A blunt needle with a large eye works best.

2. Yarn threader - assists in threading a yarn end through the eye of a needle.

3. Gauge ruler - used for measuring small areas or measuring stitches for gauge.

4. Tape measure - used for measuring stitches for gauge, taking body measurements, and measuring overall dimensions of your project.

5. Markers - used for marking the right side of your work and designating a particular stitch or row/round for later reference. In addition to split ring markers, safety pins or scrap pieces of yarn or thread also work well.

6. Bobbins - used to keep yarns from knotting together when working with small amounts of more than one color.

7. Row counter - helps to keep track of rows or rounds worked.

CROCHET BASICS

MATERIALS NEEDED FOR BEGINNERS
To learn the basics of crochet, you will need an aluminum crochet hook, size H (5.00 mm) *(see Crochet Hooks, page 2)* and a skein of worsted weight yarn *(see Yarns And Threads, page 3)*, preferably a light or bright color so your stitches will be easier to see.

LET'S BEGIN
First you need to learn how to hold a crochet hook and yarn.

Note: Instructions and figs for most of the Crochet Basics section are provided for both right-handed and left-handed crocheters. If you are left-handed, please be sure to read the special note on page 18 after you have become familiar with the basic stitches.

Holding a crochet hook and yarn will be slightly awkward at first, but with practice it will become easier and more comfortable. The hook is held in your right or left hand with the yarn and work in progress in your other hand.

HOLDING THE HOOK
The hook may be held using one of the following methods:

Method 1: You may hold the hook as you would a pencil, with the hook on top of your hand *(Fig. 8a)*.

Fig. 8a   Right-handed   Left-handed

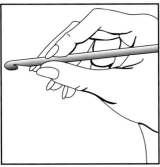

Method 2: You may grasp the hook with your fingers resting over it *(Fig. 8b)*, similar to the way you might hold a mixing spoon.

Fig. 8b   Right-handed   Left-handed

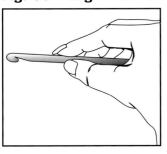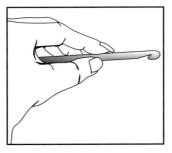

Try both methods and choose the one that feels best for you.

MAKING A SLIP KNOT
Before learning how to hold the yarn, let's start with a slip knot on the hook. Leaving a 4" length of yarn, make a circle and place the working yarn (the yarn coming from the ball or skein) under the circle *(Fig. 9a)*.

Fig. 9a   Right-handed   Left-handed

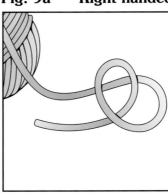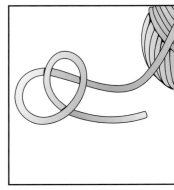

Insert the hook under the bar just made *(Fig. 9b)* onto the working area of the hook *(Fig. 1, page 2)*.

Fig. 9b   Right-handed   Left-handed

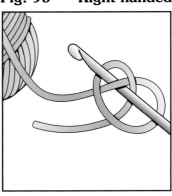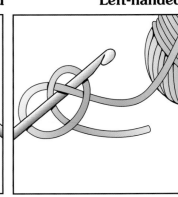

Then pull on both ends of the yarn to tighten the slip knot *(Fig. 9c)*. The loop formed should be close to the hook, but **not** tight. The loop should be able to slide easily along the working area of the hook.

Fig. 9c   Right-handed   Left-handed

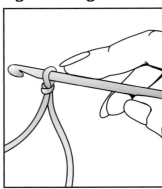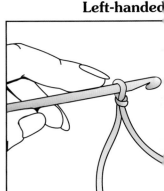

HOLDING THE YARN

Hold your hook with the slip knot in your right or left hand. Loop the working yarn over the index finger of your other hand and hold it loosely across the palm of your hand with your last two fingers, grasping the slip knot with the thumb and middle finger *(Fig. 10)*. As you crochet, you will work with the section of yarn between your index finger and the hook.

Fig. 10   Right-handed   Left-handed

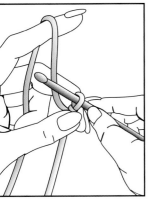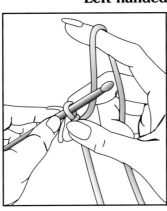

You do not have to limit yourself to this particular way of holding yarn. **If you later find that holding the yarn in a different way is easier, then feel free to do it your own way.** The important thing to remember is to allow the yarn to move smoothly and evenly through your fingers without letting it become stretched and taut.

LET'S CROCHET

Most crochet begins with a length of stitches that look like a series of V's. These stitches are called chains, and this initial group of chain stitches is referred to as the beginning or foundation chain. The first chain starts with a slip knot on the hook, then the yarn is caught by the hook in a technique called **yarn over**.

YARN OVER *(abbreviated YO)*

In addition to being part of making a chain, this technique of catching the yarn with the hook is part of every crochet stitch.

Keeping the slip knot on the hook in the working area, hold the hook in your right or left hand and the working yarn in your other hand *(Fig. 10)*.

To yarn over, bring the yarn **over** the top of the hook from back to front, catching the yarn with the hook and turning the hook slightly toward you to slip the yarn into the groove (throat) of the hook *(Fig. 11)*. This will prevent the yarn from slipping off the hook.

Fig. 11   Right-handed   Left-handed

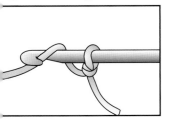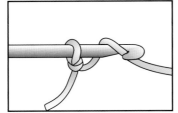

MAKING A CHAIN *(abbreviated ch)*

To complete the chain after you bring the yarn over the hook *(Fig. 11)*, simply draw the yarn through the slip knot on the hook *(Fig. 12a)* and up onto the working area of the hook. You have made one chain *(Fig. 12b)*, and one loop will remain on the hook.

Fig. 12a   Right-handed   Left-handed

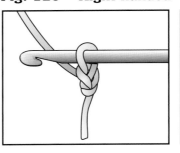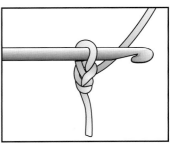

Fig. 12b   Right-handed   Left-handed

The loop formed on the hook when your chain is completed should be loose enough for the hook to go back through easily. As with the slip knot, the loop should be close to the hook, but **not** tight. This will allow the hook to pass through the chain easily when working other stitches into the chain.

Make sure that you always bring the yarn over the hook from **back** to **front** as shown in **Fig. 13a**, not from front to back as shown in **Fig. 13b**.

Fig. 13a   Right-handed   Left-handed

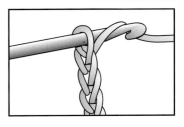

CORRECT

Fig. 13b   Right-handed   Left-handed

INCORRECT

Continued on page 7.

Note: If the hook slips out of your work, be sure to reinsert it through the front of the stitch without twisting the loop *(Fig. 14)*.

Fig. 14   Right-handed   Left-handed

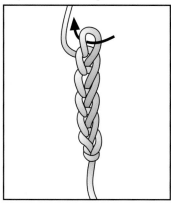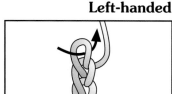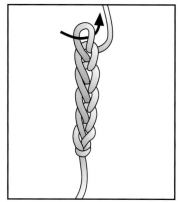

Take care to pull each new loop up onto the working area of the hook. If you work too close to the end of the hook, in the shaped area, your stitches will be too tight.

As a beginner, you may have a tendency to work tightly. Try to relax and work **loosely**. It is better to have your work too loose in the beginning than too tight. The more you practice, the better your tension (your control of the yarn) will become.

Note: If your beginning chain is continually too tight, try using a hook one size larger for making the beginning chain, then switch back to the specified hook.

ADDITIONAL CHAINS

To make each additional chain, bring yarn over the hook and draw through the loop on hook.

Remember that you **never** count the loop on the hook or the beginning slip knot as a chain stitch *(Fig. 15)*.

Fig. 15   Right-handed   Left-handed

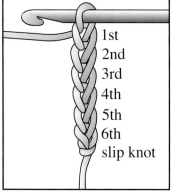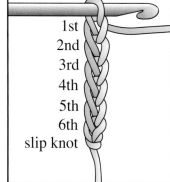

When counting chains, always begin with the first chain from the hook and then count toward the beginning of your foundation chain.

As you add stitches and the chain grows longer, move your thumb and finger closer to the hook *(Fig. 16a)*. If you work with your fingers too far down the chain *(Fig. 16b)*, you will lose control of your tension.

Fig. 16a   Right-handed   Left-handed

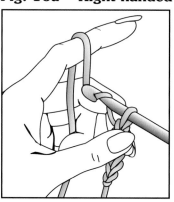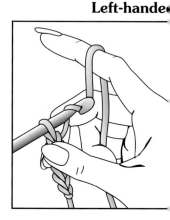

CORRECT

Fig. 16b   Right-handed   Left-handed

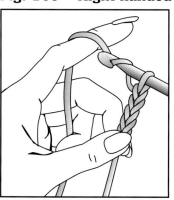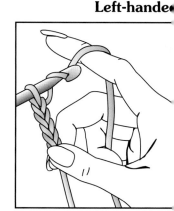

INCORRECT

Continue to add chains until you feel comfortable making a chain and your stitches are neat and even. When the chain is as long as you want it to be, cut the yarn and pull the yarn end through the last loop to secure it.

CHAINING LOOSELY

Pattern instructions almost always instruct you to crochet the beginning chain loosely (except when using cotton yarn, which stretches naturally). This is to allow for flexibility of the first row.

Here are a few ways to tell if your chains are loose enough:

1. As long as the loop formed on your hook with each chain stays the same size as the working area of the hook, the chain **will** be sufficiently loose and easy to work into.

2. If you allow the loop to shrink to the size of the hook's throat *(Fig. 1, page 2)*, it will become too tight.

3. If you have to force the hook in order to push it through a chain, then it would be best to try again and make your chain looser.

It is **very important** that the loop remains the same size as the working area of the hook you are using.

WORKING INTO THE CHAIN

When your foundation chain is complete, crochet stitches will then be worked in the individual chains. There are two different methods for doing this.

Compare the chain you made to the one in **Figs. 17a** & **b**. The front of the chain looks like a series of V's and the back of the chain has a ridge (or a bump) behind each chain stitch (called the back ridge).

Fig. 17a Right-handed   Left-handed

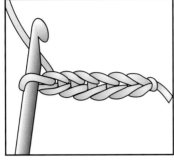

FRONT

Fig. 17b Right-handed   Left-handed

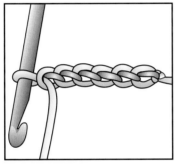

BACK

Method 1: BACK RIDGE OF A CHAIN

Insert the hook into the back ridge only of each chain (Fig. 18a).

Fig. 18a Right-handed   Left-handed

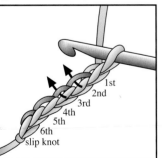

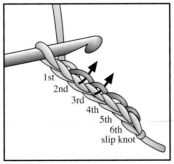

Method 2: TOP TWO LOOPS OF A CHAIN

Insert the hook under the top strand **and** the back ridge of each chain (Fig. 18b).

Fig. 18b Right-handed   Left-handed

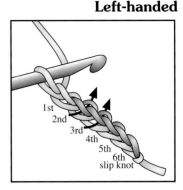

Either way is acceptable; however, working into the back ridge of a chain gives the piece a smoother edge. Some patterns will specify to use the back ridge. For those that do not, feel free to use either method. Whichever you choose, use that way consistently in any one project.

BASIC STITCHES

Now that you are familiar with holding a hook and yarn, bringing yarn over, and making a chain, learning the basic stitches (or any other stitch) is just an extension of these techniques.

In addition to the chain, most crochet designs use a combination of one or more of these five basic stitches: slip stitch, single crochet, half double crochet, double crochet, and treble crochet. These stitches are created with the same techniques used to make the chain stitch. Each stitch is made with one or more yarn overs and is completed by drawing the hook through the loop or loops on the hook, varying the height of the stitches (Fig. 19).

Fig. 19
Right-handed   Left-handed

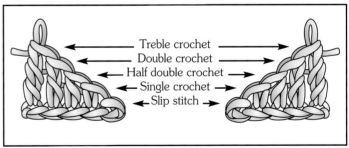

Treble crochet
Double crochet
Half double crochet
Single crochet
Slip stitch

Continued on page 9.

SINGLE CROCHET *(abbreviated sc)*

The most commonly used basic stitch is the single crochet.

To practice making single crochets, let's work a sample swatch.

ROW 1

Chain 17 stitches **loosely** *(Figs. 12a & b, page 6)*.

Step 1: Insert hook in the **second** chain from the hook *(Figs. 18a or b, page 8)*.

Step 2: Bring yarn over *(Fig. 11, page 6)* and pull up a loop through the chain *(Fig. 20a)* but not through the loop on the hook. You now have 2 loops on the hook.

Fig. 20a Right-handed   **Left-handed**

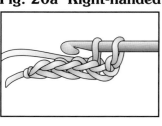

Step 3: Bring yarn over and draw through **both** loops on the hook *(Fig. 20b)*.

Fig. 20b Right-handed   **Left-handed**

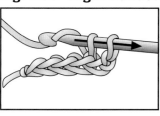

You have made one single crochet *(Fig. 20c)*, and one loop will remain on the hook.

Fig. 20c Right-handed   **Left-handed**

Note: As you crochet, you will always have one loop remaining on your hook at the completion of a stitch.

Step 4: Insert hook in the next chain.

Step 5: Bring yarn over and pull up a loop (2 loops on hook).

Step 6: Bring yarn over and draw through both loops on the hook **(single crochet made)**.

Repeat Steps 4-6 in each chain across, taking care not to twist the foundation chain as you work.

You should now have one row of 16 single crochets. Notice the top of the row of single crochets. Each single crochet has two horizontal strands (loops) that look like horizontal V (similar to a chain). These are the loops you will work into for the next row.

To begin the next row of single crochets, you must first make a **turning chain** to raise the yarn to the height of a single crochet, and then turn the work around so you can crochet back across the first row.

The turning chain for a single crochet is one chain. This chain is used **only** to gain row height; we do not count this chain as the first single crochet.

ROW 2

Step 1: Chain one stitch *(Fig. 21, turning chain made)*.

Fig. 21   Right-handed   **Left-handed**

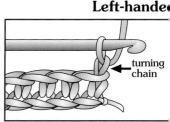

Step 2: Turn your work around *(Fig. 22)*.

Fig. 22   Right-handed   **Left-handed**

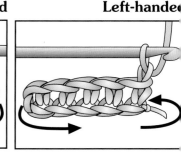

Step 3: Insert the hook **under both** top loops of the first single crochet (the single crochet closest to the hook) *(Fig. 23)*.

Fig. 23   Right-handed   **Left-handed**

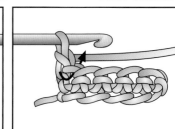

Step 4: Bring yarn over and pull up a loop (2 loops on hook).

Step 5: Bring yarn over and draw through both loops on the hook **(single crochet made)**.

Step 6: Work a single crochet in each of the remaining single crochets across the row. You should still have 6 single crochets.

Make sure you worked into the last single crochet of the row *(Fig. 24)*.

Fig. 24   Right-handed   Left-handed

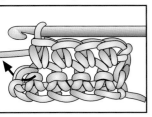 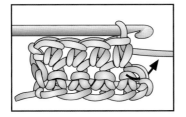

ROW 3

Repeat Steps 1-6 of Row 2; do **not** work into the turning chain since it does not count as a stitch when working single crochets *(Fig. 25)*.

Fig. 25   Right-handed   Left-handed

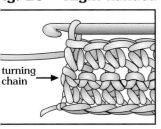 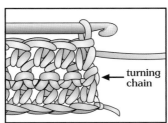

turning chain →   ← turning chain

Continue practicing rows of single crochets until you are comfortable with these steps. **Fig. 26** shows a swatch of single crochets. Before finishing your swatch, let's learn another important basic stitch, the slip stitch.

Fig. 26   Right-handed

Left-handed

SLIP STITCH *(abbreviated slip st)*

This stitch is used to attach new yarn, to join work, or to move the yarn across a group of stitches without adding height.

Let's practice making slip stitches.

Step 1: Turn your work, then insert hook **under both** top loops of the first single crochet *(Figs. 22 & 23, page 9)*. Bring yarn over *(Fig. 11, page 6)* and draw through the stitch **and** the loop on the hook *(Fig. 27a)*.

Fig. 27a   Right-handed   Left-handed

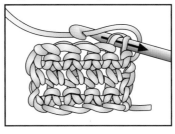 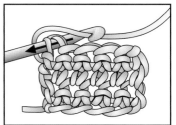

You have made one slip stitch *(Fig. 27b)*, and one loop will remain on the hook.

Fig. 27b   Right-handed   Left-handed

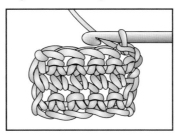 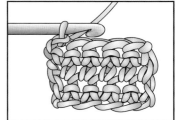

Step 2: Insert hook in the next single crochet, bring yarn over and draw through the stitch **and** the loop on the hook **(slip stitch made)**.

Repeat Step 2 in each single crochet across; then follow the next section to finish off your yarn.

FINISH OFF

When you complete your last stitch, cut the yarn leaving a 4-6" end. Bring the loose end through the last loop on your hook and tighten it *(Fig. 28)*.

Fig. 28   Right-handed   Left-handed

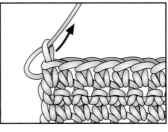 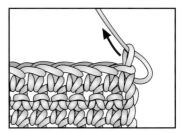

This secures the end so the stitches won't unravel. This technique is referred to as **finish off**, **fasten off**, or **end off** in most instructions.

If you find that your yarn is too slippery or stiff to stay secure with this ending, then make an extra chain after your last stitch and pull the loose end through that chain.

HALF DOUBLE CROCHET
(abbreviated hdc)

This stitch is slightly taller than a single crochet.

To practice making half double crochets, let's work another sample swatch.

ROW 1
Chain 17 stitches **loosely** *(Figs. 12a & b, page 6)*.

Step 1: Bring yarn over *(Fig. 11, page 6)* and insert hook in the **third** chain from the hook *(Fig. 29a)*, keeping the new loop (the yarn over) on the hook.

Fig. 29a   Right-handed   Left-handed

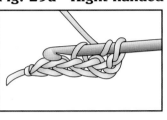

Step 2: Bring yarn over and pull up a loop through the chain *(Fig. 29b)* but not through the loops on the hook. You now have 3 loops on the hook.

Fig. 29b   Right-handed   Left-handed

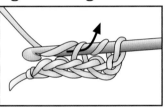

Step 3: Bring yarn over and draw through **all** 3 loops on the hook at once *(Fig. 29c)*.

Fig. 29c   Right-handed   Left-handed

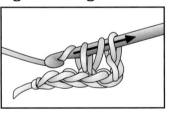

You have made one half double crochet *(Fig. 29d)*, and one loop will remain on the hook.

Fig. 29d   Right-handed   Left-handed

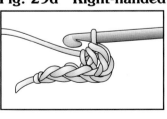

Step 4: Bring yarn over and insert hook in the next chain.

Step 5: Bring yarn over and pull up a loop (3 loops on hook).

Step 6: Bring yarn over and draw through all 3 loops on the hook **(half double crochet made)**.

Repeat Steps 4-6 across the chain.

You should have 15 half double crochets plus the two chains at the beginning of the row (which count as one stitch) for a total of 16 stitches.

To begin the next row of half double crochets, you must first make a **turning chain** to raise the yarn to the height of a half double crochet, and then turn the work around so you can crochet back across the first row.

The turning chain for a half double crochet is two chains. These chains serve two purposes; they gain row height **and** count as the first half double crochet of the row.

ROW 2
Step 1: Chain 2 stitches, then turn your work around *(Fig. 30, turning chain made) (counts as first half double crochet)*.

Fig. 30   Right-handed   Left-handed

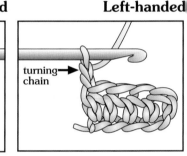

Step 2: Bring yarn over, skip the first half double crochet and insert the hook **under both** top loops of the next half double crochet *(Fig. 31)*.

Fig. 31   Right-handed   Left-handed

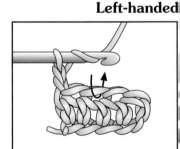

Step 3: Bring yarn over and pull up a loop (3 loops on hook).

Step 4: Bring yarn over and draw through all 3 loops on the hook **(half double crochet made)**.

Step 5: Work a half double crochet in each of the remaining half double crochets across the row, working the last half double crochet in top of the beginning chain *(Fig. 32)*.

Fig. 32   **Right-handed**   **Left-handed**

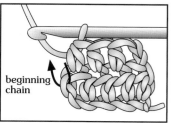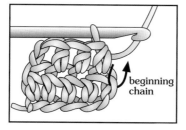

Counting the turning chain, you now have 16 half double crochets.

ROW 3
Repeat Steps 1-5 of Row 2, working the last half double crochet into the turning chain *(Fig. 33)*.

Fig. 33   **Right-handed**   **Left-handed**

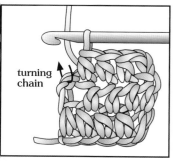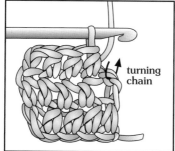

Continue practicing rows of half double crochets until you are comfortable with these steps, then finish off your work *(Fig. 28, page 10)*. **Fig. 34** shows a swatch of half double crochets.

Fig. 34   **Right-handed**

Left-handed

DOUBLE CROCHET
(abbreviated dc)
This stitch is made in the same manner as a half double crochet with one additional step. A double crochet is slightly taller than a half double crochet and twice as tall as a single crochet.

Let's work another swatch and practice making double crochets.

ROW 1
Chain 18 stitches **loosely** *(Figs. 12a & b, page 6)*.

Step 1: Bring yarn over *(Fig. 11, page 6)* and insert hook in the **fourth** chain from the hook *(Fig. 35a)*, keeping the new loop on the hook.

Fig. 35a   Right-handed   **Left-handed**

Step 2: Bring yarn over and pull up a loop through the chain *(Fig. 35b)* but not through the loops on the hook. You now have 3 loops on the hook.

Fig. 35b   Right-handed   **Left-handed**

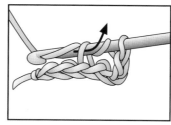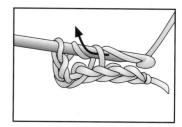

Step 3: Bring yarn over and draw through the **first** 2 loops on the hook *(Fig. 35c)*. You now have 2 loops remaining on the hook.

Fig. 35c   Right-handed   **Left-handed**

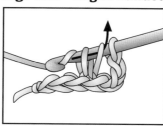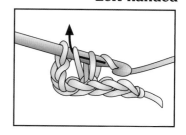

Continued on page 13.

Step 4: Bring yarn over and draw through the **remaining** 2 loops on the hook *(Fig. 35d)*.

Fig. 35d   Right-handed   Left-handed

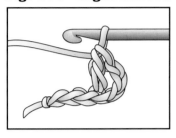 

You have made one double crochet *(Fig. 35e)*, and one loop will remain on the hook.

Fig. 35e   Right-handed   Left-handed

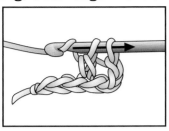 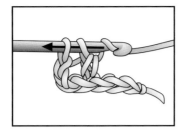

Step 5: Bring yarn over and insert hook in the next chain.

Step 6: Bring yarn over and pull up a loop (3 loops on hook).

Step 7: Bring yarn over and draw through the first 2 loops on the hook (2 loops remain on hook).

Step 8: Bring yarn over and draw through the remaining 2 loops on the hook **(double crochet made)**.

Repeat Steps 5-8 across the chain.

You should have 15 double crochets plus the three chains at the beginning of the row (which count as one stitch) for a total of 16 stitches.

To begin the next row of double crochets, you must first make a **turning chain** to raise the yarn to the height of a double crochet, and then turn the work around so you can crochet back across the first row.

The turning chain for a double crochet is three chains. These chains provide row height **and** count as the first double crochet of the row.

ROW 2
Step 1: Chain 3 stitches, then turn your work around *(Fig. 36, turning chain made) (counts as first double crochet)*.

Fig. 36   Right-handed   Left-handed

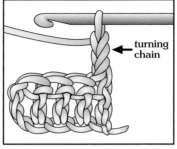 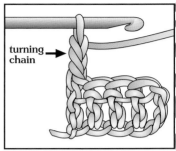

Step 2: Bring yarn over, skip the first double crochet and insert the hook **under both** top loops of the next double crochet *(Fig. 37)*.

Fig. 37   Right-handed   Left-handed

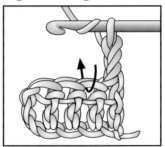 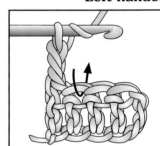

Step 3: Bring yarn over and pull up a loop (3 loops on hook).

Step 4: Bring yarn over and draw through the first 2 loops on the hook (2 loops remain on hook).

Step 5: Bring yarn over and draw through the remaining 2 loops on the hook **(double crochet made)**.

Step 6: Work a double crochet in each of the remaining double crochets across the row, working the last double crochet in top of the beginning chain *(Fig. 38)*.

Fig. 38   Right-handed   Left-handed

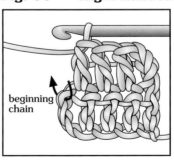 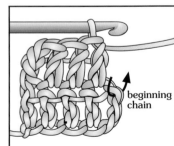

Counting the turning chain, you now have 16 double crochets.

ROW 3

Repeat Steps 1-6 of Row 2, working the last double crochet into the turning chain *(Fig. 33, page 12)*.

Continue practicing rows of double crochets until you are comfortable with these steps, then finish off your work *(Fig. 28, page 10)*. **Fig. 39** shows a swatch of double crochets.

Fig. 39   **Right-handed**

Left-handed

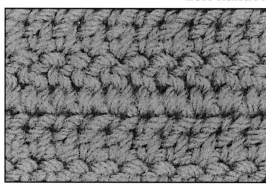

TREBLE CROCHET *(abbreviated tr)*

The treble crochet is taller than all the previous stitches you have learned.

Let's make another practice swatch while we learn how to work treble crochets.

ROW 1

Chain 19 stitches **loosely** *(Figs. 12a & b, page 6)*.

Step 1: Bring yarn over **twice** *(Fig. 11, page 6)* and insert hook in the **fifth** chain from the hook *(Fig. 40a)*, keeping both new loops on the hook.

Fig. 40a   Right-handed   **Left-handed**

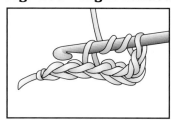
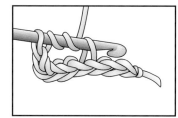

Step 2: Bring yarn over and pull up a loop through the chain *(Fig. 40b)* but not through the loops on the hook. You now have 4 loops on the hook.

Fig. 40b   Right-handed   **Left-handed**

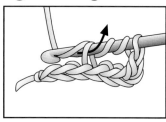
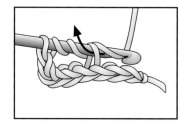

Step 3: Bring yarn over and draw through the **first** 2 loops on the hook *(Fig. 40c)*. You now have 3 loops remaining on the hook.

Fig. 40c   Right-handed   **Left-handed**

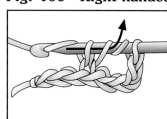
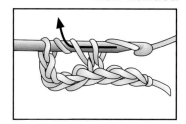

Continued on page 15.

14

Step 4: Bring yarn over and draw through the **next** 2 loops on the hook *(Fig. 40d)*. You now have 2 loops remaining on the hook.

Fig. 40d   Right-handed   Left-handed

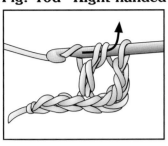

Step 5: Bring yarn over and draw through the **remaining** 2 loops on the hook *(Fig. 40e)*.

Fig. 40e   Right-handed   Left-handed

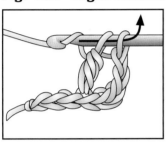

You have made one treble crochet *(Fig. 40f)*, and one loop will remain on the hook.

Fig. 40f   Right-handed   Left-handed

Step 6: Bring yarn over twice and insert hook in the next chain.

Step 7: Bring yarn over and pull up a loop (4 loops on hook).

Step 8: Bring yarn over and draw through the first 2 loops on the hook (3 loops remain on hook).

Step 9: Bring yarn over and draw through the next 2 loops on the hook (2 loops remain on hook).

Step 10: Bring yarn over and draw through the remaining 2 loops on the hook **(treble crochet made)**.

Repeat Steps 6-10 across the chain.

You should have 15 treble crochets plus the four chains at the beginning of the row (which count as one stitch) for a total of 16 stitches.

To begin the next row of treble crochets, you must first make a **turning chain** to raise the yarn to the height of a treble crochet, and then turn the work around so you can crochet back across the first row.

The turning chain for a treble crochet is four chains. These chains provide row height **and** count as the first treble crochet of the row.

ROW 2
Step 1: Chain 4 stitches, then turn your work around *(Fig. 41,* **turning chain made) (counts as first treble crochet)**.

Fig. 41   Right-handed   Left-handed

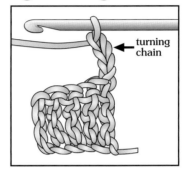

Step 2: Bring yarn over twice, skip the first treble crochet and insert the hook **under both** top loops of the next treble crochet *(Fig. 42)*.

Fig. 42   Right-handed   Left-handed

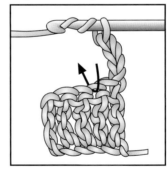

Step 3: Bring yarn over and pull up a loop (4 loops on hook).

Step 4: Bring yarn over and draw through the first 2 loops on the hook (3 loops remain on hook).

Step 5: Bring yarn over and draw through the next 2 loops on the hook (2 loops remain on hook).

Step 6: Bring yarn over and draw through the remaining 2 loops on the hook **(treble crochet made)**.

15

Step 7: Work a treble crochet in each of the remaining treble crochets across the row, working the last treble crochet in top of the beginning chain *(Fig. 43)*.

Fig. 43   **Right-handed**   **Left-handed**

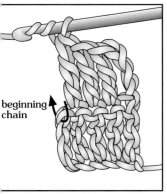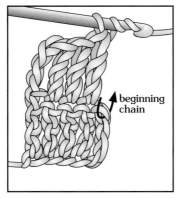

beginning chain

beginning chain

Counting the turning chain, you now have 6 treble crochets.

ROW 3
Repeat Steps 1-7 of Row 2, working the last treble crochet into the turning chain *(Fig. 33, page 12)*.

Continue practicing rows of treble crochets until you are comfortable with these steps, then finish off your work *(Fig. 28, page 10)*. **Fig. 44** shows a swatch of treble crochets.

Fig. 44   **Right-handed**

Left-handed

TURNING CHAINS

As explained in each of the basic stitches, a chain or a group of chains called the turning chain is needed at the beginning of each row or round to gain the height necessary for making your next stitch.

Remember, the turning chain must be equal in height to the stitch you are going to use in a particular row or round *(Fig. 45)*.

Fig. 45
Right-handed   **Left-handed**

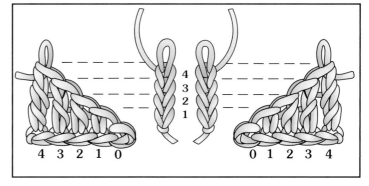

0 - Slip stitch
1 - Single crochet
2 - Half double crochet
3 - Double crochet
4 - Treble crochet

A slip stitch adds no height, so it does not need a turning chain.

A single crochet is the same height as one chain. This one turning chain gains row or round height **only**; it does **not** count as the first single crochet.

A half double crochet is the same height as two chains, a double crochet is the same height as three chains, and a treble crochet is the same height as four chains. For these taller stitches, the turning chain usually counts as the first stitch of that row or round.

ROWS AND ROUNDS

All pieces of crochet are worked in either rows or rounds.

WORKING IN ROWS

To work in rows, you almost always start with a beginning chain. After working the first row across the beginning chain, you will make a turning chain and turn the piece around to work back across the stitches on the first row. Stitches are worked back and forth across the piece, turning it at the beginning of each row.

WORKING IN ROUNDS

When working in rounds, crochet is worked in a circular fashion instead of back and forth in rows. The following are variations of working in rounds.

MAKING A BEGINNING LOOP

A beginning loop starts with a beginning chain, and all the stitches for the first round are worked into the last chain from the hook. **Fig. 46** shows one example, a chain-4 with double crochets worked in the fourth chain from the hook.

Fig. 46   **Right-handed**   **Left-handed**

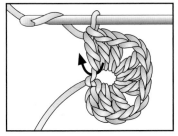
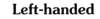
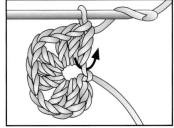

MAKING A BEGINNING RING

A beginning ring is used when you need more stitches on the first round than a beginning loop will hold. To form a beginning ring, work the specified number of chains and then join to the first chain made with a slip stitch **(Fig. 47)**. This method will leave an open center and stitches may be worked either in the actual ring or in the chains. If stitches will be worked in the chains, be careful not to twist the chain when joining.

Fig. 47   **Right-handed**   **Left-handed**

CONTINUOUS ROUNDS

Continuous rounds are primarily used in single crochet and are worked without joining or turning (in a continuous spiral fashion) **(Fig. 48)**. To keep track of rounds, a marker is placed at the beginning of each round and is moved after each round is complete **(see Markers, page 22)**.

Fig. 48   **Right-handed**   **Left-handed**

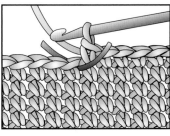
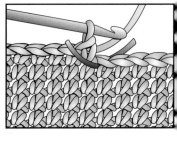

ROUNDS WITHOUT TURNING

In this technique, the yarn is joined with a slip stitch **(Figs. 27a & b, page 10)** to the top of the beginning chain or to the first stitch of each round, but the piece is **not** turned at the beginning of the next round. Note that with this method there is a definite visible joining line which moves slightly upward toward the right or left in a spiral **(Fig. 49)**. This cannot be avoided and is the reason garments are often designed in two pieces with side seams rather than worked in rounds.

Fig. 49   **Right-handed**   **Left-handed**

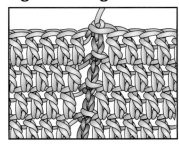
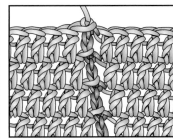

ROUNDS WITH TURNING

For rounds with turning, the yarn is joined with a slip stitch **(Figs. 27a & b, page 10)** to the top of the beginning chain or to the first stitch of each round, and then the piece is turned at the beginning of the next round. The visible joining line will remain straight in this method **(Fig. 50)**.

Fig. 50   **Right-handed**   **Left-handed**

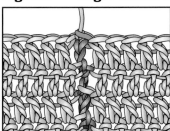
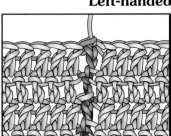

SPECIAL NOTE TO LEFT-HANDED CROCHETERS

Now that you have become familiar with the basics of crochet, take a few minutes to compare the differences between the figs you have been using and the right-handed figs. Notice that the only differences are the way the stitches lean and the direction in which the stitches are worked. You can accomplish any pattern stitch if you remember that you will work the mirror image of all right-handed figs. All the steps will be worked in exactly the same manner; you will simply be working in the opposite direction.

When making a garment, you will also encounter a difference in shaping. Since most instructions are written for right-handed crocheters, the pieces you make will be a mirror image. For example, a piece labeled Right Front in instructions will actually become your Left Front, and vice versa.

Just remember that you crochet from **left** to **right** instead of right to left like right-handed crocheters, so it may be necessary for you to occasionally reverse some instructions.

*Note: The remaining instructions and figs will reflect the **right-handed** version.*

ADDITIONAL TECHNIQUES

Here are a variety of techniques and stitch variations you will encounter as you crochet.

ADDING NEW YARN AND CHANGING COLORS

Whether you are adding new yarn or simply changing colors, there are several methods for accomplishing this change. Whenever possible, attach new yarn at the **end** of a row or round by joining within the last stitch.

JOINING WITHIN A STITCH

This method of attaching yarn, whether to change color or simply add new yarn, may be used in the **middle** or at the **end** of a row or round.

Work the last stitch to within one step of completion, hook the new yarn (*Figs. 51a or b*), and draw through all loops on the hook. Cut old yarn and work over both ends unless indicated otherwise.

Fig. 51a

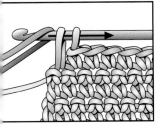

Fig. 51b

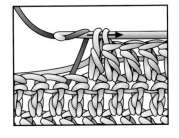

JOINING WITH SLIP STITCH

Begin with a slip knot on your hook (*Figs. 9a-c, page 5*). Insert hook in the stitch or space indicated, yarn over (*Fig. 11, page 6*) and draw through the stitch or space **and** the loop on the hook (*Figs. 52a & b*).

Fig. 52a

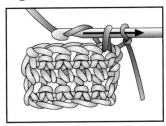

Fig. 52b

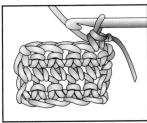

JOINING WITH SINGLE CROCHET

Begin with a slip knot on your hook (*Figs. 9a-c, page 5*). Insert hook in the stitch or space indicated, yarn over (*Fig. 11, page 6*) and pull up a loop, yarn over and draw through both loops on the hook (*Figs. 53a & b*).

Fig. 53a

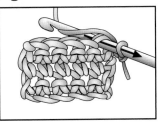

Fig. 53b

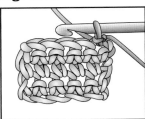

BACK OR FRONT LOOP ONLY

Work only in the loop(s) indicated by arrow (*Fig. 54*).

Fig. 54

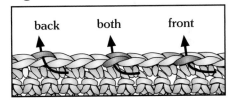

BACK OR FRONT POST STITCHES

Work around the post of stitch indicated, inserting the hook in direction of arrow (*Fig. 55*).

Fig. 55

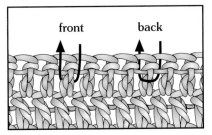

FREE LOOPS

After working in the Back or Front Loops Only on a row or round *(Fig. 54, page 18)*, there will be a ridge of unused loops. These are called the free loops. Later, when instructed to work in the free loops of the same row or round, work in these loops *(Fig. 56a)*.

When instructed to work in the free loops of a chain, work in loop indicated by arrow *(Fig. 56b)*.

Fig. 56a

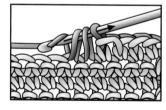

Fig. 56b

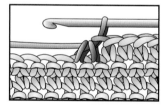

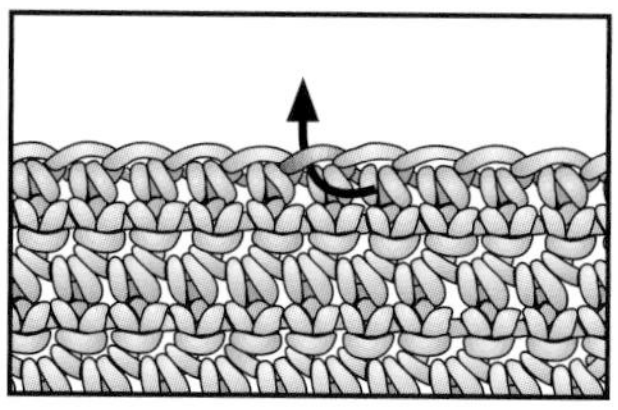

DECREASES

Decreases are used for shaping. They reduce the number of stitches and make the piece narrower.

When a decrease is used in a pattern stitch, the instructions are usually included for that specific decrease. Each basic stitch, however, has its own method of decreasing by combining two stitches into one.

SINGLE CROCHET DECREASE

(abbreviated sc decrease)

Insert hook in **next** stitch, yarn over *(Fig. 11, page 6)* and pull up a loop (2 loops on hook), insert hook in **next** stitch, yarn over and pull up a loop (3 loops on hook), yarn over *(Fig. 57a)* and draw through **all** 3 loops on the hook at once *(Fig. 57b, single crochet decrease made)*. The decrease counts as one single crochet.

Fig. 57a

Fig. 57b

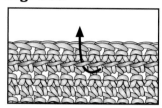

Note: You may also complete a single crochet decrease by simply skipping a stitch. However, this is **not** recommended for the remaining basic stitches, because undesirable holes will be created.

HALF DOUBLE CROCHET DECREASE

(abbreviated hdc decrease)

Yarn over *(Fig. 11, page 6)*, insert hook in **next** stitch, yarn over and pull up a loop (3 loops on hook), yarn over, insert hook in **next** stitch, yarn over and pull up a loop (5 loops on hook), yarn over *(Fig. 58a)* and draw through **all** 5 loops on the hook at once *(Fig. 58b, half double crochet decrease made)*. The decrease counts as one half double crochet.

Fig. 58a

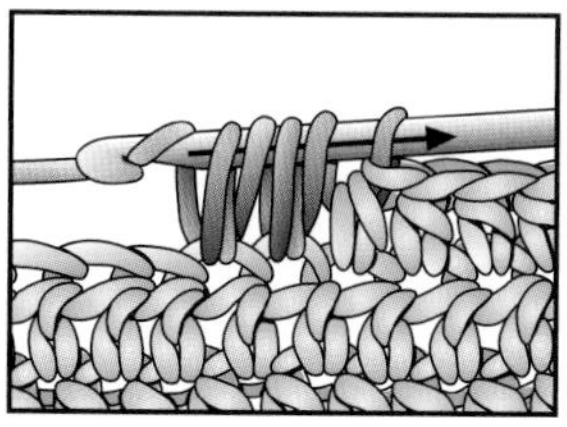

Fig. 58b

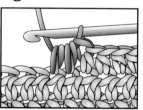

DOUBLE CROCHET DECREASE

(abbreviated dc decrease)

Yarn over *(Fig. 11, page 6)*, insert hook in **next** stitch, yarn over and pull up a loop, yarn over and draw through first 2 loops on hook (2 loops remaining on hook), yarn over, insert hook in **next** stitch, yarn over and pull up a loop, yarn over and draw through next 2 loops on hook (3 loops remaining on hook), yarn over *(Fig. 59a)* and draw through **all** 3 loops on the hook at once *(Fig. 59b, double crochet decrease made)*. The decrease counts as one double crochet.

Fig. 59a

Fig. 59b

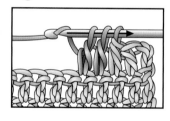

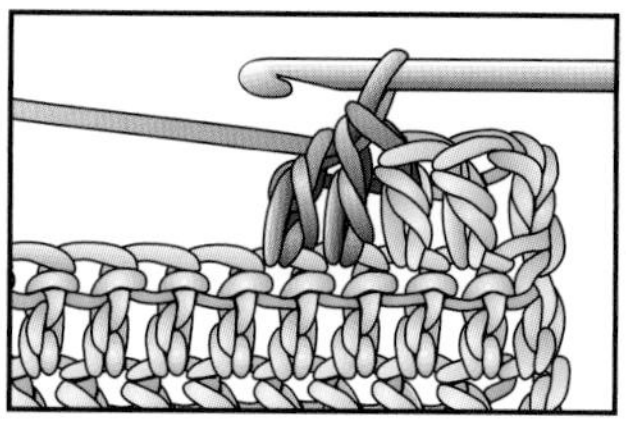

TREBLE CROCHET DECREASE

(abbreviated tr decrease)

Yarn over twice *(Fig. 11, page 6)*, insert hook in **next** stitch, yarn over and pull up a loop, yarn over and draw through first 2 loops on hook, yarn over and draw through next 2 loops on hook (2 loops remaining on hook), yarn over twice, insert hook in **next** stitch, yarn over and pull up a loop, yarn over and draw through first 2 loops on hook, yarn over and draw through next 2 loops on hook (3 loops remaining on hook), yarn over *(Fig. 60a)* and draw through **all** 3 loops on the hook at once *(Fig. 60b, treble crochet decrease made)*. The decrease counts as one treble crochet.

Fig. 60a

Fig. 60b

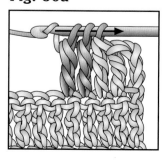

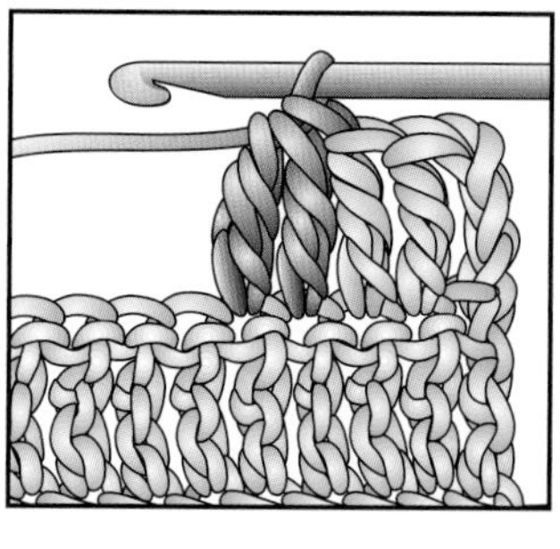

INCREASES

Increases are used to add stitches to enlarge a circle, create shaping to make a piece wider, or to round corners.

An increase is the addition of a stitch so that you have two stitches worked into one stitch. To ease around a corner, there may be an increase of three stitches worked into the same stitch.

Whether you are working a single crochet, half double crochet, double crochet, or treble crochet, the increase will be made by working two or more of the same stitch into a single stitch or space. For example, **Fig. 61** shows a single crochet increase.

Fig. 61

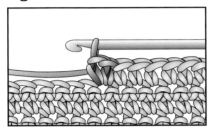

When an increase is used in a pattern stitch, the instructions are usually included for that specific increase.

ADDING ON SINGLE CROCHET

When instructed to add on a single crochet at the end of a row, insert hook into the base of last single crochet made *(Fig. 62)*, yarn over *(Fig. 11, page 6)* and pull up loop, yarn over and draw through one loop on hook, yarn over and draw through both loops on hook **(single crochet added on)**. Repeat as many times as instructed.

Fig. 62

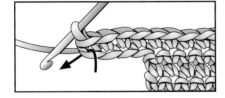

RIGHT OR WRONG SIDE

The **right** side of your work (the side that will show) is generally a matter of personal preference, but the suggested right side will usually be indicated in the pattern instructions. If right side is not denoted in instructions, then follow the guidelines listed below:

1. When working in rounds without turning, the side facing you as you work is always the "right" side.
2. When working in rows, the last row usually determines the "right" side.

Please refer to the photographs below. Both are the same piece photographed from different sides. Photo A shows the "right" side facing; Photo B shows the "wrong" side.

Notice the very smooth edge on the piece in Photo A, then compare that to the bumpy edge in Photo B. That smooth edge (the last round), clearly defined in Photo A, denotes the "right" side.

Photo A **Right side**

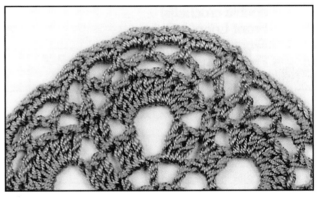

Photo B **Wrong side**

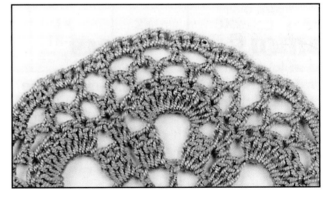

UNDERSTANDING INSTRUCTIONS

Crochet instructions are written in a special language consisting of abbreviations, punctuation marks, and other terms and symbols. This method of writing saves time and space, and is actually easy to read once you understand the crochet shorthand.

A list of abbreviations will be included with each leaflet or pattern, and you should review this list carefully before beginning a project. The abbreviations, symbols, and terms most frequently used by *Leisure Arts* are listed below.

ABBREVIATIONS

BLO	Back Loop(s) Only
BP	Back Post
BPdc	Back Post double crochet(s)
BPtr	Back Post treble crochet(s)
CC	Contrasting Color
ch(s)	chain(s)
dc	double crochet(s)
FLO	Front Loop(s) Only
FP	Front Post
FPdc	Front Post double crochet(s)
FPtr	Front Post treble crochet(s)
hdc	half double crochet(s)
LSC	Long Single Crochet(s)
MC	Main Color
mm	millimeters
Rnd(s)	Round(s)
sc	single crochet(s)
sp(s)	space(s)
st(s)	stitch(es)
tr	treble crochet(s)
YO	yarn over

SYMBOLS AND TERMS

★ — used to shorten instructions. Work all instructions following a ★ (star) as many **more** times as indicated in addition to the first time.

† **to** † — used to shorten instructions. Work all instructions from the first † (dagger) to the second † **as many** times as specified.

multiple — the number of stitches required to complete one repeat of a pattern.

post — the vertical shaft of a stitch.

right vs. left — the side of the garment as if you were wearing it.

right side vs. wrong side — the **right** side of your work is the side that will show when the piece is finished.

work across or around — continue working in the established pattern.

CROCHET TERMINOLOGY	
UNITED STATES	**INTERNATIONAL**
slip stitch (slip st)	= single crochet (sc)
single crochet (sc)	= double crochet (dc)
half double crochet (hdc)	= half treble crochet (htr)
double crochet (dc)	= treble crochet (tr)
treble crochet (tr)	= double treble crochet (dtr)
double treble crochet (dtr)	= triple treble crochet (ttr)
skip	= miss

PUNCTUATION

When reading crochet instructions, read from punctuation mark to punctuation mark. Just as in grammar, commas (,) mean pause and semicolons (;) mean stop.

colon (:) — the number(s) given after a colon at the end of a row or round denote(s) the number of stitches you should have on that row or round.

braces { } — contain information pertaining to multiple sizes.

parentheses ( ) or brackets [ ] — indicate repetition, so you should work the enclosed instructions **as many** times as specified by the number immediately following. For example, when instructions read "[sc in next 2 sts, ch 3, (work Popcorn in next st, ch 3) twice] 4 times," the instructions within the parentheses are repeated twice and the entire sequence enclosed by brackets is repeated a total of four times. Parentheses or brackets may also indicate that several stitches are to be worked as a unit, so you should work all enclosed instructions in the stitch or space indicated. For example, when instructions read "(sc, 2 dc, sc) in next ch-2 sp," **all** the stitches within the parentheses should be worked into the next ch-2 sp. Parentheses or brackets may also contain explanatory remarks.

READING PATTERNS

Let's see how crochet instructions look when written in abbreviated form. Below are two examples of instructions. Under each example, a "translation" of how to read the example is given.

Instructions — Ch 28 **loosely**.

Translation — Make a slip knot *(Figs. 9a-c, page 5)*, then make 28 chain stitches *(Figs. 12a & b, page 6)* that are loose enough to work back into *(see Chaining Loosely, page 7)*.

Instructions — **Row 1** (Right side)**:** Dc in fourth ch from hook **(3 skipped chs count as first dc)**, skip next ch, sc in next ch, ★ skip next ch, 3 dc in next ch, skip next ch, sc in next ch; repeat from ★ across to last 2 chs, skip next ch, 2 dc in last ch: 25 sts.

Translation — Make one double crochet in the fourth chain from the hook *(Figs. 35a-e, pages 12 & 13)*. (Note that the three chains you just skipped will count as the first double crochet of the row). Skip the next chain, then make one single crochet in the next chain *(Figs. 20a-c, page 9)*. ★ Skip the next chain, make three double crochets in the next chain, skip the next chain, and make one single crochet in the next chain; repeat each step after the ★ (all the instructions between the star and the semi-colon) across the chain until only two chains remain. Skip the next chain and make two double crochets in the last chain. You now have a total o 25 stitches.

GAUGE

Gauge is the number of stitches and rows or rounds per inch and is used to determine the finished size. All crochet patterns will specify the gauge that you must match to ensure proper size and to be sure you have enough yarn to complete the project.

Because everyone crochets differently - loosely, tightly, or somewhere in between - the finished size can vary even when crocheters use the very same pattern, yarn, and hook.

Before beginning any crocheted item, it is absolutely necessary for you to crochet a gauge swatch in the pattern stitch with the weight of yarn and hook size suggested. Your swatch must be large enough to measure your gauge, usually 4" square.

The following is an example of a gauge swatch.

YARN: Worsted weight *(see Yarns And Threads, page 3)*

HOOK: Size H (5.00 mm) *(see Crochet Hooks, page 2)*

GAUGE: 16 single crochets and 16 rows = 4"

Gauge Swatch: (4" x 4")
Chain 17 **loosely** *(Figs. 12a & b, page 6)*.
Row 1: Single crochet in second chain from hook *(Figs. 20a-c, page 9)* and in each chain across: 16 single crochets.
Rows 2-16: Chain 1, turn *(Figs. 21 & 22, page 9)*; single crochet in each single crochet across. Finish off *(Fig. 28, page 10)*.

Lay your swatch on a hard, smooth, flat surface. Then measure to see if it measures 4" x 4".
If it is **smaller** than 4", you are crocheting too tightly - try again with a **larger** size hook.
If it is **larger** than 4", you are crocheting too loosely - try again with a **smaller** size hook.
Keep trying until your swatch measures 4" x 4".

Making an accurate gauge swatch **each** time you begin a project takes time, but crocheting an item that is too small or too large is a waste of time and money.

Once you have obtained the correct gauge, you should continue to measure the total width of your work every three to four inches to be sure your gauge does not change. Remember, it is your responsibility to make sure you are matching the gauge indicated in the pattern. DO NOT HESITATE TO CHANGE HOOK SIZE IN ORDER TO MAINTAIN CORRECT GAUGE.

MARKERS

Markers are used as important reminders in a pattern *(see Additional Accessories, page 4)*.

Continuous Rounds: Markers are used to help distinguish the beginning of each round being worked. Place a marker before the first stitch of each round, moving marker after each round is complete.

Right Side: When instructed to place a marker to indicate the right side, loop a short piece of yarn around any stitch on the side facing **before** the work is turned.

Stitch Placement: When instructed to place a marker around a particular stitch for stitch placement (on a later row or round), be careful to mark the correct stitch. If you work in a stitch other than the one that should have been marked, the instructions may not work on the following rows or rounds.

MEASURING UP

SIZING
DECIDING WHICH SIZE TO CROCHET
Most garment patterns are written for at least three different sizes. Instructions usually include actual chest/bust measurement or generic size (small, medium, large) and the finished measurement of the garment, which usually allows several inches for ease.

MEASURING FOR SIZE
Chest/Bust: Measure around the fullest part of the chest/bust, keeping tape under arms and around shoulder blades.

MEN'S

	X-Small	Small	Medium	Large
Chest	30-32"	34-36"	38-40"	42-44"
	X-Large		XX-Large	
Chest	46-48"		50-52"	

WOMEN'S

	X-Small	Small	Medium	Large
Size Bust	4 33"	6-8 34-35"	10-12 36-37½"	14-16 38-40½"
Size Bust	1X 18-20 42-45½"	2X 22-24 46-49½"	3X 26-28 50-53½"	4X 30-32 54-57½"

You may want to measure a favorite sweater with similar styling, and crochet the size that has the nearest finished measurement.

INFANTS AND CHILDREN
The only accurate way to determine which size to crochet for a child is to measure the child.

MEASURING YOUR CROCHET
Many instructions include schematics (or drawings) of the garment. The finished measurements of each piece are indicated for your reference so that you may accurately measure your work.

Always measure your crochet on a hard, smooth, flat surface such as a table or uncarpeted floor. Measure each piece along the lines indicated on the schematics, being careful not to stretch or bunch the piece.

GETTING IT TOGETHER

The assembly and finishing of a design should be done with great care. A crocheted item can be ruined by sloppy or incorrect finishing. The following techniques will add value and beauty to your finished work.

WEAVING IN YARN ENDS

Good finishing techniques make a big difference in the quality of any crocheted piece. Make a habit of taking care of loose ends as you work. **Never** tie a knot in your yarn. They may poke through to the right side and will sometimes come untied and unravel. Weaving in the ends gives a much better result. Thread a yarn needle with the yarn end. With **wrong** side facing, weave the needle through several stitches, then reverse the direction and weave it back through several more stitches. When the end is secure, clip the yarn off close to your work.

You may also hide your ends as you work by crocheting over them for several inches to secure; clip the remaining lengths off close to your work.

Always check your work to be sure the yarn ends do not show on the right side.

SEAMS

A tapestry or yarn needle is best to use for sewing seams because the blunt point will not split the yarn. Use the same yarn the item was made with to sew the seams. However, if the yarn is textured or bulky, it may be easier to sew the seam with a small, smooth yarn of the same color, such as tapestry yarn or an acrylic needlepoint yarn. If a different yarn is used for the seams, be sure the care instructions for both yarns are the same. If the yarn used to crochet the item is machine washable, the seam yarn must also be machine washable.

Any of the following techniques may be used for joining seams; however, it is usually best to weave the side and underarm seams of a garment because weaving is practically invisible and does not add bulk.

WEAVING

With **right** side of both pieces facing you and edges even, sew through both pieces once to secure the beginning of the seam, leaving an ample yarn end to weave in later. Insert the needle from **right** to **left** through one strand on each piece *(Fig. 63)*. Bring the needle around and insert it from **right** to **left** through the next strand on both pieces. Continue in this manner, drawing seam together as you work.

Fig. 63

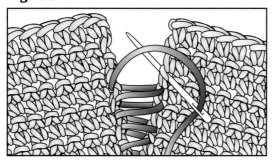

BACKSTITCH

Backstitch provides a firm seam. With **right** sides together and edges even, weave yarn end in securely. Insert the needle from **front** to **back** at the edge of the seam, then bring it up from **back** to **front** a half stitch forward (at 1). ★ Insert the needle back where the first stitch began (at 2) and bring it up a whole stitch forward (at 3) *(Fig. 64a)*. Insert the needle a half stitch back from the yarn (at 1) and up again a whole stitch forward (at 4) *(Fig. 64b)*. Repeat from ★ across the seam.

Fig. 64a

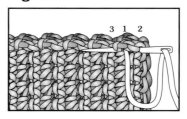

Fig 64b

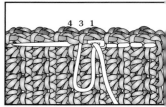

WHIPSTITCHING

Whipstitching can be accomplished from either the right or wrong sides, inside loops or both loops, and from front to back or back to front. Pattern instructions should specify the type of whipstitching to be used on a particular design. The following are just a few of the possibilities.

WHIPSTITCH ACROSS END OF ROWS

With **right** sides together, sew through both pieces once to secure the beginning of the seam, leaving an ample yarn end to weave in later. Insert the needle from **back** to **front** through one strand on each piece *(Fig. 65)*. Bring the needle around and insert it from **back** to **front** through the next strand on both pieces. Repeat along the edge, being careful to match stitches and rows.

Fig. 65

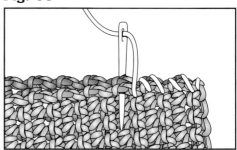

23

WHIPSTITCH IN BOTH LOOPS

Place two Motifs, Squares, or Strips with **wrong** sides together. Beginning in first corner, sew through both pieces once to secure the beginning of the seam, leaving an ample yarn end to weave in later. Working through **both** loops of each stitch of **both** pieces, insert the needle from **back** to **front** through first stitch and pull yarn through *(Fig. 66)*, ★ insert the needle from **back** to **front** through next stitch and pull yarn through; repeat from ★ across to next corner.

Fig. 66

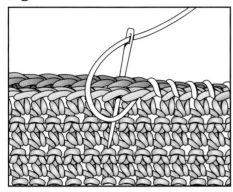

WHIPSTITCH IN INSIDE LOOPS

Place two Motifs, Squares, or Strips with **wrong** sides together. Beginning in first corner, sew through both pieces once to secure the beginning of the seam, leaving an ample yarn end to weave in later. Working through **inside** loop of each stitch of **both** pieces, insert the needle from **front** to **back** through first stitch and pull yarn through *(Fig. 67)*, ★ insert the needle from **front** to **back** through next stitch and pull yarn through; repeat from ★ across to next corner.

Fig. 67

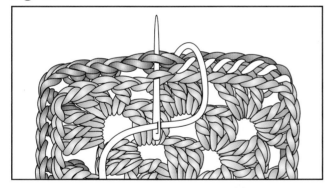

EDGING
SINGLE CROCHET EVENLY ACROSS OR AROUND

When you are instructed to single crochet evenly across or around, the single crochets should be spaced to keep the piece lying flat. Work a few single crochets at a time, checking periodically to be sure your edge is not distorted. If the edge is puckering, you need to add a few more single crochets; if the edge is ruffling, you need to remove some single crochets. Keep trying until the edge lies smooth and flat.

BLOCKING

Blocking "sets" a crocheted item and smoothes the stitches to give your work a professional appearance. Before blocking, check the yarn label for any special instructions because many acrylics and some blends may be damaged during blocking.

Note: Always use rust-proof pins.

On fragile acrylics that can be blocked, you simply pin your item to the correct size on a towel-covered board, and cover the item with dampened bath towels. When the towels are dry, the item is blocked.

If the item is hand washable, carefully launder it using a mild soap or detergent. Rinse it without wringing or twisting. Remove any excess moisture by rolling it in a succession of dry towels. If you prefer, you may put it in the final spin cycle of your washer - but do not use water or heat. Lay the item on a large towel on a flat surface out of direct sunlight. Gently smooth and pat it to the desired size and shape, comparing the measurements to the pattern instructions as necessary. When the item is completely dry, it is blocked.

Steaming is an excellent method of blocking crochet items, especially those made with wool or wool blends. Turn the item **wrong** side out and pin it to the correct size on a board covered with towels. Hold a steam iron or steamer just above the item and steam it thoroughly. Never let the weight of the iron touch your item because it will flatten the stitches. Leave the garment pinned until it is completely dry.

FRINGE

Cut a piece of cardboard 3" wide and ½" longer than you want your finished fringe to be. Wind the yarn **loosely** and **evenly** around the cardboard lengthwise until the card is filled, then cut across one end; repeat as needed.

Hold together half as many strands of yarn as desired for the finished fringe; fold in half.

With **wrong** side facing and using a crochet hook, draw the folded end up through a stitch or space and pull the loose ends through the folded end *(Fig. 68a)*; draw the knot up **tightly** *(Fig. 68b)*. Repeat, spacing as desired. Lay flat on a hard surface and trim the ends.

Fig. 68a

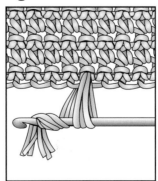

Fig. 68b

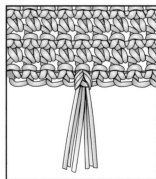

pages 31-32

pages 29-30

page 33

page 30

REVERSIBLE AFGHAN

Photographs on covers and page 25.

Finished Size: Approximately 48" x 67"

ABBREVIATIONS
See Understanding Instructions, page 21.

MATERIALS
Solid Only
Worsted Weight Yarn, approximately:
58 ounces, (1,650 grams, 3,645 yards)
Crochet hook, size H (5.00 mm) **or** size needed for gauge
Multicolored Only
Worsted Weight Yarn, approximately:
Color A (Ecru) - 15 ounces,
(430 grams, 1,115 yards)
Color B (Light Blue) - 14 ounces,
(400 grams, 1,040 yards)
Color C (Blue) - 15 ounces,
(430 grams, 1,115 yards)
Color D (Dark Blue) - 13 ounces,
(370 grams, 965 yards)
Crochet hook, size P (10.00 mm) **or** size needed
for gauge

GAUGE: For Multicolored Only, 9 sts and 6 rows = 4"
For Solid Only, 15 sts and 10 rows = 4"

Note: Multicolored Afghan is worked holding **two** strands of yarn together, and Solid Afghan is worked holding only **one** strand.

Instructions are written for Multicolored Afghan with instructions for Solid Afghan in braces { }. If only one number is given, it applies to both Afghans.

On either Afghan, each row is worked across length of Afghan.

Multicolored ONLY
Color Sequence: One row Color A *(Fig. 51a, page 18)*, 2 rows **each**: Color B, Color C, Color D, ★ Color A, Color B, Color C, Color D; repeat from ★ 7 times **more**, then work one row Color A.

Ch 150{252} **loosely** *(Figs. 12a & b, page 6)*.

Row 1 (Right side)**:** Sc in back ridge of second ch from hook *(Fig. 18a, page 8, and Figs. 20a-c, page 9)* and each ch across: 149{251} sc.

Note: Loop a short piece of yarn around any stitch to mark last row as **right** side.

Row 2: Ch 1, turn; sc in first sc, [dc in next sc *(Figs. 35a-e, pages 12 & 13)*, sc in next sc] across: 149{251} sts.

Row 3: Ch 1, turn; working in Back Loops Only *(Fig. 54, page 18)*, sc in first sc, (dc in next dc, sc in next sc) across.

Row 4: Ch 1, turn; working in both loops, sc in first sc (dc in next dc, sc in next sc) across.

Rows 5-71{119}: Repeat Rows 3 and 4, 33{57} times; then repeat Row 3 once **more**.

Row 72{120}: Ch 1, turn; sc in both loops of each st across; finish off *(Fig. 28, page 10)*.

With corresponding colors and using 6{4} 16" strands for each fringe, add fringe evenly across short edges of Afghan *(Figs. 68a & b, page 24)*.

Design by Jennine Korejko.

BABY AFGHAN

Photographs on covers.

Finished Size: Approximately 35" x 44"

ABBREVIATIONS
See Understanding Instructions, page 21.

MATERIALS
Sport Weight Yarn, approximately:
MC (Yellow) - 11 ounces,
(310 grams, 1,035 yards)
Color A (White) - 7½ ounces,
(210 grams, 705 yards)
Color B (Blue) - 3 ounces,
(90 grams, 285 yards)
Crochet hook, size G (4.00 mm) **or** size needed
for gauge
Yarn needle

GAUGE: Each Square = 4¼"

SQUARE (Make 80)
With Color B (Blue), ch 6 *(Figs. 12a & b, page 6)*; join with slip st to form a ring *(Figs. 27a & b, page 10, and Fig. 47, page 17)*.

Rnd 1 (Right side)**:** Ch 1, ★ 3 sc in ring *(Figs. 20a-c, page 9)*, ch 4; repeat from ★ 3 times **more**; join with slip st to first sc: 12 sc and 4 ch-4 sps.

Note: Loop a short piece of yarn around any stitch to mark last round as **right** side.

Rnd 2: Ch 1, sc in same st and in next 2 sc, (slip st, ch 9, slip st) in next ch-4 sp, ★ sc in next 3 sc, (slip st, ch 9, slip st) in next ch-4 sp; repeat from ★ 2 times **more**; join with slip st to first sc, finish off *(Fig. 28, page 10)*: 12 sc and 4 loops (ch-9).

Rnd 3: With **right** side facing and working **behind** loop, join Color A (White) with slip st in any ch-4 sp on Rnd 1 *(Figs. 52a & b, page 18)*; ch 3 **(counts as first dc, now and throughout)**, (dc, ch 2, 2 dc) in same sp *(Figs. 35a-e, pages 12 & 13)*, dc in next 3 sc on Rnd 2, ★ working **behind** next loop, (2 dc, ch 2, 2 dc) in next ch-4 sp on Rnd 1, dc in next 3 sc on Rnd 2; repeat from ★ around; join with slip st to first dc: 28 dc and 4 ch-2 sps.

Rnd 4: Ch 3, dc in next dc, 2 dc in next ch-2 sp, dc in next loop on **Rnd 2**, ch 9, slip st in top of dc just made, 2 dc in same sp on **Rnd 3**, dc in next 2 dc, ch 3, skip next 3 dc, ★ dc in next 2 dc, 2 dc in next ch-2 sp, dc in next loop on **Rnd 2**, ch 9, slip st in top of dc just made, 2 dc in same sp on **Rnd 3**, dc in next 2 dc, ch 3, skip next 3 dc; repeat from ★ around; join with slip st to first dc, finish off: 36 dc and 4 loops.

To work **Front Post treble crochet** *(abbreviated FPtr)*, YO twice *(Fig. 11, page 6)*, insert hook from **front** to **back** around post of dc indicated, YO and pull up a loop, (YO and draw through 2 loops on hook) 3 times *(Fig. 69)*.

Fig. 69

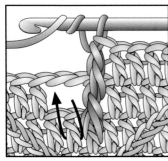

Rnd 5: With **right** side facing, join MC (Yellow) with slip st in same st as joining; ch 3, dc in next 3 dc, working **behind** next loop, (2 dc, ch 1, 2 dc) in same dc as loop, dc in next 4 dc, working in **front** of next ch-3, work FPtr around each of next 3 skipped dc on **Rnd 3** *(Fig. 69)*, ★ dc in next 4 dc on **Rnd 4**, working **behind** next loop, (2 dc, ch 1, 2 dc) in same dc as loop, dc in next 4 dc, working in **front** of next ch-3, work FPtr around each of next 3 skipped dc on **Rnd 3**; repeat from ★ around; join with slip st to first dc: 60 sts and 4 ch-1 sps.

Rnd 6: Ch 1, sc in same st and in next 5 dc, sc in next ch-1 sp, sc in next loop on **Rnd 4** and in same sp on **Rnd 5**, ★ sc in next 15 sts and in next ch-1 sp, sc in next loop on **Rnd 4** and in same sp on **Rnd 5**; repeat from ★ 2 times **more**, sc in each st across; join with slip st to first sc, finish off: 72 sc.

FINISHING
ASSEMBLY
With MC (Yellow) and working through **inside** loops, whipstitch Squares together forming 8 vertical strips of 10 Squares each *(Fig. 67, page 24)*, beginning in center sc of first corner and ending in center sc of next corner; then whipstitch strips together in same manner.

EDGING
Rnd 1: With **right** side facing, join MC (Yellow) with sc in any corner sc *(Figs. 53a & b, page 18)*; 2 sc in same st, sc evenly around working 3 sc in each corner sc *(see Edging, page 24)*; join with slip st to first sc.

Rnd 2: Ch 1, working from **left** to **right**, ★ insert hook in sc to right of hook *(Fig. 70a)*, YO and draw through, under and to left of loop on hook (2 loops on hook) *(Fig. 70b)*, YO and draw through both loops on hook *(Fig. 70c)* **(reverse sc made, Fig. 70d)**; repeat from ★ around; join with slip st to first st, finish off.

Fig. 70a

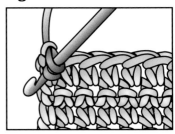

Fig. 70b

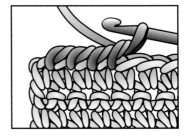

Fig. 70c

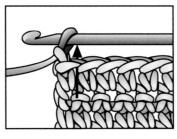

Fig. 70d

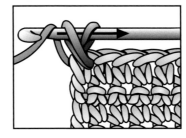

VEST

Photographs on covers and page 26.

Size	Finished Chest Measurement
Small	40"
Medium	44"
Large	48"

Size Note: Instructions are written for size Small with sizes Medium and Large in braces { }. Instructions will be easier to read if you circle all the numbers pertaining to your size. If only one number is given, it applies to all sizes.

ABBREVIATIONS
See Understanding Instructions, page 21.

MATERIALS
Sport Weight Yarn, approximately:
- **Solid Only**
  - MC (Blue) - 8½{9-10½} ounces, [240{260-300} grams, 850{900-1,050} yards]
  - CC (Dark Blue) - ½ ounce, (20 grams, 50 yards)
- **Striped Only**
  - MC (Dark Blue) - 5{5½-6} ounces, [140{160-170} grams, 500{550-600} yards]
  - CC (Red) - 4{4-5} ounces, [110{110-140} grams, 400{400-500} yards]
- Crochet hook, size E (3.50 mm) **or** size needed for gauge
- Yarn needle

GAUGE: 18 sc and 22 rows = 4"

STRIPED VEST COLOR SEQUENCE
SIZE SMALL ONLY
8 Rows **each**: MC *(Fig. 51a, page 18)*, (CC, MC) 6 times.
SIZES MEDIUM AND LARGE ONLY
8 Rows **each**: MC *(Fig. 51a, page 18)*, (CC, MC) 6 times, 4{7} rows CC.

BODY
Note: For Solid Vest, use MC throughout.

Ch 181{199-217} **loosely** *(Figs. 12a & b, page 6)*.

Row 1 (Right side): Sc in second ch from hook *(Figs. 20a-c, page 9)* and in each ch across: 180{198-216} sc.

Note: Loop a short piece of yarn around any stitch to mark last row as **right** side.

Rows 2-52: Ch 1, turn; sc in each sc across.

Do **not** finish off.

RIGHT FRONT
Row 53: Ch 1, turn; sc in first 38{43-48} sc, leave remaining 142{155-168} sc unworked.

Rows 54 and 55: Ch 1, turn; sc in each sc across to last 2 sc, skip next sc, sc in last sc: 36{41-46} sc.

Row 56: Ch 1, turn; sc in each sc across.

Rows 57-59: Ch 1, turn; sc in each sc across to last 2 sc, skip next sc, sc in last sc: 33{38-43} sc.

Rows 60-63: Repeat Rows 56-59: 30{35-40} sc.

Rows 64 and 65: Ch 1, turn; sc in each sc across.

Row 66: Ch 1, turn; sc in each sc across to last 2 sc, skip next sc, sc in last sc: 29{34-39} sc.

Rows 67-69: Ch 1, turn; sc in each sc across.

Rows 70 thru 90{98-106}: Repeat Rows 66-69, 5{7-9} times; then repeat Row 66 once **more**: 23{26-29} sc.

Rows 91{99-107} thru 104{108-111}: Ch 1, turn; sc in each sc across.

Finish off leaving a long end for sewing *(Fig. 28, page 10)*.

BACK
Row 53: With **right** side facing and working in unworked sc on Row 52, skip first 12 sc from Right Front and join yarn with sc in next sc *(Figs. 53a & b, page 18)*; sc in next 79{87-95} sc, leave remaining 50{55-60} sc unworked: 80{88-96} sc.

Row 54: Ch 1, turn; sc in each sc across.

Row 55: Ch 1, turn; skip first sc, sc in next sc and in each sc across to last 2 sc, skip next sc, sc in last sc: 78{86-94} sc.

Rows 56-63: Repeat Rows 54 and 55, 4 times: 70{78-86} sc.

Rows 64 thru 104{108-111}: Ch 1, turn; sc in each sc across.

Finish off.

LEFT FRONT
Row 53: With **right** side facing and working in unworked sc on Row 52, skip first 12 sc from Back and join yarn with sc in next sc; sc in each sc across: 38{43-48} sc.

Rows 54 and 55: Ch 1, turn; skip first sc, sc in next sc and in each sc across: 36{41-46} sc.

Row 56: Ch 1, turn; sc in each sc across.

Rows 57-59: Ch 1, turn; skip first sc, sc in next sc and in each sc across: 33{38-43} sc.

Rows 60-63: Repeat Rows 56-59: 30{35-40} sc.

Rows 64 and 65: Ch 1, turn; sc in each sc across.

Row 66: Ch 1, turn; skip first sc, sc in next sc and in each sc across: 29{34-39} sc.

Rows 67-69: Ch 1, turn; sc in each sc across.

ows 70 thru 90{98-106}: Repeat Rows 66-69,
{7-9} times; then repeat Row 66 once **more**:
3{26-29} sc.

ows 91{99-107} thru 104{108-111}: Ch 1,
rn; sc in each sc across.

nish off leaving a long end for sewing.

ew shoulder seams **(Fig. 63, page 23)**.

DGING

o work **Long Single Crochet (abbreviated LSC)**,
sert hook in sc 2 rows **below** next sc **(Fig. 71a) or** in
cond sc **below** sc at end of next row **(Fig. 71b)**, YO
Fig. 11, page 6) and pull up a loop even with loop on
ook, YO and draw through both loops on hook.

Fig. 71a

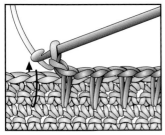

Fig. 71b

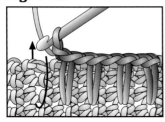

OLID VEST

Body: With **right** side facing, join CC with slip st in any
c at center of Back neck edge **(Figs. 52a & b,**
age 18); ch 1, (work LSC, ch 1) evenly around working
SC, ch 1) 3 times in each corner **(see Edging,**
age 24, and Figs. 71a & b); join with slip st to first
SC **(Figs. 27a & b, page 10)**, finish off.

rmhole: With **right** side facing, join CC with slip st in
ny sc at underarm; ch 1, (work LSC, ch 1) evenly
round; join with slip st to first LSC, finish off.

epeat for second Armhole.

TRIPED VEST

Body: With **right** side facing, join MC with sc in any sc
t center of Back neck edge; sc evenly around working
sc in each corner **(see Edging, page 24)**; join with
lip st to first sc **(Figs. 27a & b, page 10)**, finish off.

rmhole: With **right** side facing, join MC with sc in any
c at underarm; sc evenly around; join with slip st to first
c, finish off.

epeat for second Armhole.

Design by Margie Wicker.

COASTERS
Photographs on front cover and page 26.

Finished Size: Approximately 4½" in diameter

ABBREVIATIONS
See Understanding Instructions, page 21.

MATERIALS
Bedspread Weight Cotton Thread (size 10),
approximately 25 yards for **each** Coaster
Steel crochet hook, size 6 (1.80 mm) **or** size
needed for gauge

GAUGE: Rnds 1-3 = 2"

Ch 6 **(Figs. 12a & b, page 6)**; join with slip st to
form a ring **(Figs. 27a & b, page 10, and Fig. 47,
page 17)**.

Rnd 1 (Right side)**:** Ch 3 **(counts as first dc, now
and throughout)**, 23 dc in ring **(Figs. 35a-e,
pages 12 & 13)**; join with slip st to first dc: 24 dc.

Rnd 2: Ch 5, skip next dc, ★ dc in next dc, ch 2, skip
next dc; repeat from ★ around; join with slip st to third
ch of beginning ch-5: 12 ch-2 sps.

Rnd 3: Slip st in first ch-2 sp, ch 3, 2 dc in same sp,
ch 1, 3 dc in next ch-2 sp, ch 6, ★ 3 dc in next ch-2 sp,
ch 1, 3 dc in next ch-2 sp, ch 6; repeat from ★ around;
join with slip st to first dc: 6 loops (ch-6) and 6 ch-1 sps.

Rnd 4: Slip st in next 2 dc and in next ch-1 sp, ch 3, dc
in same sp, 10 dc in next loop, (2 dc in next ch-1 sp,
10 dc in next loop) around; join with slip st to first dc:
72 dc.

Rnd 5: Ch 1, sc in same st and in next dc **(Figs. 20a-c,
page 9)**, ch 3, (skip next dc, sc in next dc, ch 3) twice,
★ skip next 2 dc, (sc in next dc, ch 3, skip next dc) twice,
sc in next 2 dc, ch 3, (skip next dc, sc in next dc, ch 3)
twice; repeat from ★ around to last 6 dc, skip next 2 dc,
sc in next dc, ch 3, skip next dc, sc in next dc, ch 1, hdc
in first sc to form last ch-3 sp **(Figs. 29a-d, page 11)**:
30 ch-3 sps.

Rnd 6: Ch 1, sc in same sp, (ch 3, sc in next ch-3 sp)
around, ch 1, hdc in first sc to form last ch-3 sp.

Rnd 7: Ch 1, sc in same sp, ch 10, skip next ch-3 sp,
★ sc in next ch-3 sp, ch 10, skip next ch-3 sp; repeat
from ★ around; join with slip st to first sc:
15 loops (ch-10).

To work **Picot**, ch 3, slip st in third ch from hook.

Rnd 8: Slip st in first loop, ch 1, (6 sc, work Picot, 6 sc)
in same loop and in each loop around; join with slip st to
first sc, finish off **(Fig. 28, page 10)**.

Design by Nair Carswell.

KOALA BEAR

Photographs on front cover and page 25.

Finished Size: Approximately 8½" high

ABBREVIATIONS
See Understanding Instructions, page 21.

MATERIALS
Worsted Weight Yarn, approximately:
    MC (Tan) - 3 ounces, (90 grams, 200 yards)
    Color A (White) - 25 yards
    Color B (Black) - 10 yards
Crochet hook, size H (5.00 mm) **or** size needed
    for gauge
Polyester stuffing
Yarn needle

GAUGE: Rnds 1-3 of Head = 1½"
            7 sc and 7 rows = 2"

HEAD
With MC (Tan), ch 3 **loosely** *(Figs. 12a & b, page 6)*; being careful not to twist ch, join with slip st to form a ring *(Figs. 27a & b, page 10, and Fig. 47, page 17)*.

Rnd 1 (Right side)**:** 2 Sc in each ch around *(Figs. 20a-c, page 9)*; do **not** join, place marker *(see Continuous Rounds, page 17, and Markers, page 22)*: 6 sc.

Rnd 2: 2 Sc in each sc around: 12 sc.

Rnd 3: (Sc in next sc, 2 sc in next sc) around: 18 sc.

Rnd 4: (Sc in next 2 sc, 2 sc in next sc) around: 24 sc.

Rnd 5: (Sc in next 3 sc, 2 sc in next sc) around: 30 sc.

Rnd 6: (Sc in next 4 sc, 2 sc in next sc) around: 36 sc.

Rnds 7-16: Sc in each sc around.

To **decrease**, pull up a loop in each of next 2 sc, YO and draw through all 3 loops on hook *(Figs. 57a & b, page 19)* **(counts as one sc).**

Rnd 17: Decrease around; do **not** finish off: 18 sc.

Stuff Head firmly.

BODY
Rnd 1: Sc in each sc around: 18 sc.

Rnd 2: 2 Sc in each sc around: 36 sc.

Rnd 3: (Sc in next 5 sc, 2 sc in next sc) around: 42 sc.

Rnds 4-19: Sc in each sc around.

Rnd 20: (Sc in next 5 sc, decrease) around: 36 sc.

Rnd 21: Decrease around: 18 sc.

Rnd 22: Sc in each sc around.

Rnd 23: (Sc in next sc, decrease) around: 12 sc.

Rnd 24: Sc in each sc around.

Stuff Body firmly.

Rnd 25: Decrease around; slip st in next sc, finish off leaving a long end for sewing *(Fig. 28, page 10)*: 6 sc.

Thread yarn needle with end and weave through remaining stitches; gather tightly and secure.

EAR (Make 2)
INNER EAR
With Color A (White), ch 11 **loosely.**

Row 1 (Right side)**:** Sc in second ch from hook and in each ch across: 10 sc.

Row 2: Ch 1, turn; work 2 Loop Sts in first sc *(Figs. 72a-c, page 32)*, work Loop St in each sc across to last sc, work 2 Loop Sts in last sc: 12 Loop Sts.

Row 3: Ch 1, turn; sc in each st across.

Row 4: Ch 1, turn; work Loop St in first sc, skip next sc, work Loop St in next 8 sc, skip next sc, work Loop St in last sc; finish off: 10 Loop Sts.

OUTER EAR
With MC (Tan), ch 11 **loosely.**

Row 1 (Right side)**:** Sc in second ch from hook and in each ch across: 10 sc.

Note: Loop a short piece of yarn around any stitch to mark last row as **right** side.

Row 2: Ch 1, turn; 2 sc in first sc, sc in each sc across to last sc, 2 sc in last sc: 12 sc.

Row 3: Ch 1, turn; sc in each sc across.

Row 4: Ch 1, turn; decrease, sc in each sc across to last 2 sc, decrease; do **not** finish off: 10 sc.

Edging (Joining rnd)**:** With **wrong** sides together, Inner Ear facing, working through both pieces, and matching sts, 2 sc in end of each row across; 2 sc in each free loop of beginning ch *(Fig. 56b, page 19)*; 2 sc in end of each row across; sc in each st across Row 4; join with slip st to first sc, finish off leaving a long end for sewing.

Using photo as a guide for placement, sew Ears to Head.

LEG (Make 2)

With MC (Tan), ch 3 **loosely**; being careful not to twist ch, join with slip st to form a ring.

Rnd 1 (Right side)**:** 2 Sc in each ch around; do **not** join, place marker: 6 sc.

Rnd 2: 2 Sc in each sc around: 12 sc.

Rnd 3: (Sc in next sc, 2 sc in next sc) around: 18 sc.

Rnd 4: (Sc in next 2 sc, 2 sc in next sc) around: 24 sc.

Rnds 5-12: Sc in each sc around.

Rnd 13: (Sc in next 7 sc, 2 sc in next sc) around: 27 sc.

Rnd 14: (Sc in next 8 sc, 2 sc in next sc) around; slip st in next sc, finish off leaving a long end for sewing.

Using photo as a guide for placement, stuff Legs firmly and sew to Body, spacing approximately 2" apart in front.

ARM (Make 2)

With MC (Tan), ch 3 **loosely**; being careful not to twist ch, join with slip st to form a ring.

Rnd 1 (Right side)**:** 2 Sc in each ch around; do **not** join, place marker: 6 sc.

Rnd 2: 2 Sc in each sc around: 12 sc.

Rnd 3: (Sc in next sc, 2 sc in next sc) around: 18 sc.

Rnds 4-12: Sc in each sc around; at end of Rnd 12, slip st in next sc, finish off leaving a long end for sewing.

Stuff Arms firmly up to 1" from top edge; lightly stuff remaining portion.

Flatten top edge of each Arm and sew opening closed. Using photo as a guide for placement, sew Arms to Body.

NOSE

Row 1: With Color B (Black), ch 2, 2 sc in second ch from hook.

Row 2 (Right side)**:** Ch 1, turn; 2 sc in each sc across: sc.

Note: Mark last row as **right** side and top.

Rows 3-5: Ch 1, turn; sc in each sc across.

Row 6: Ch 1, turn; decrease twice: 2 sc.

Edging: Ch 1, do **not** turn; sc in end of each row across; sc in free loop of ch at base of first sc; sc in end of each row across; sc in each sc across Row 6; join with slip st to first sc, finish off leaving a long end for sewing.

Using photo as a guide for placement, sew Nose to Head, stuffing firmly before closing.

FINISHING

Using photo as a guide for placement and 2 strands of Color B (Black), embroider eyes on Head and 3 claws over end of each Leg and Arm, using 2 straight stitches for each eye and claw.

Design by Cindy Harris.

LOOP STITCH *(abbreviated Loop St)*

Insert hook in next st, wrap yarn around index finger of left hand 2 times **more**, insert hook through all loops on finger following direction indicated by arrow *(Fig. 72a)*, carefully hook all loops *(Fig. 72b)*, draw through st, remove finger from loops, YO and draw through all 4 loops on hook pulling each loop to measure approximately 1" **(Loop St made,** *Fig. 72c).*

Fig. 72a

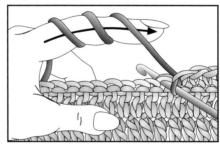

Fig. 72b

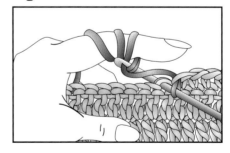

Fig. 72c

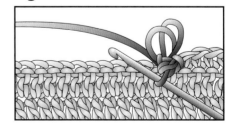

SCARF
Photograph on page 26.

Finished Size: Approximately 7" x 41"

ABBREVIATIONS
See Understanding Instructions, page 21.

MATERIALS
Worsted Weight Yarn, approximately:
MC (Green) - 3 ounces,
(90 grams, 190 yards)
Color A (Beige) - 2 ounces,
(60 grams, 125 yards)
Color B (Rust) - 2 ounces,
(60 grams, 125 yards)
Crochet hook, size H (5.00 mm) **or** size needed
for gauge

GAUGE: 13 sts and 18 rows = 4"

With MC (Green), ch 23 **loosely** *(Figs. 12a & b, page 6).*

Row 1 (Right side)**:** Sc in back ridge of second ch from hook *(Fig. 18a, page 8, and Figs. 20a-c, page 9)* and each ch across changing to Color A (Beige) in last sc *(Fig. 51a, page 18)*: 22 sc.

Note: Loop a short piece of yarn around any stitch to mark last row as **right** side.

To work **Long Single Crochet (abbreviated LSC)**, working **around** next sc, insert hook in st one row **below**, YO *(Fig. 11, page 6)* and pull up a loop even with loop on hook, YO and draw through both loops on hook *(Fig. 73)*. Skip sc under LSC.

Fig. 73

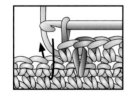

Row 2: Ch 1, turn; sc in first 2 sc, [work LSC *(Fig. 73)*, sc in next sc] across changing to Color B (Rust) in last sc.

Row 3: Ch 1, turn; sc in first 2 sc, (work LSC, sc in next st) across changing to MC (Green) in last sc.

Row 4: Ch 1, turn; sc in first 2 sc, (work LSC, sc in next st) across changing to Color A (Beige) in last sc.

Repeat Rows 2-4 until Scarf measures approximately 40" from beginning ch, ending by working Row 3; do **not** finish off.

Last Row: Ch 1, turn; sc in first 2 sc, (work LSC, sc in next sc) across; finish off *(Fig. 28, page 10)*.

With MC (Green) and using four 16" strands for each fringe, add fringe evenly across short edges of Scarf *(Figs. 68a & b, page 24)*.

DISHCLOTH
Photographs on covers.

Finished Size: Approximately 10½" x 10"

ABBREVIATIONS
See Understanding Instructions, page 21.

MATERIALS
100% Cotton Worsted Weight Yarn,
approximately:
Solid Only
2½ ounces, (70 grams, 125 yards)
Multicolored Only
MC (White) -1¼ ounces,
(40 grams, 65 yards)
CC (Yellow) - 1¼ ounces,
(40 grams, 65 yards)
Crochet hook, size H (5.00 mm) **or** size needed
for gauge

GAUGE: 12 hdc and 7 rows = 3"

Multicolored ONLY
Color Sequence: 2 Rows **each:** CC *(Fig. 51a, page 18)*, (MC, CC) 5 times changing to MC at end of Row 22.

Ch 41 **loosely** *(Figs. 12a & b, page 6).*

Row 1 (Right side)**:** Hdc in third ch from hook *(Figs. 29a-d, page 11)* **(2 skipped chs count as first hdc)** and in each ch across: 40 hdc.

Rows 2-22: Ch 2 **(counts as first hdc)**, turn; ★ hdc in Back Loop Only of next hdc *(Fig. 54, page 18)*, hdc in Front Loop Only of next hdc; repeat from ★ across to last hdc, hdc in last hdc.

Do **not** finish off.

EDGING
Rnd 1: Ch 1, turn; 3 sc in first hdc *(Figs. 20a-c, page 9)*, sc in each hdc across to last hdc, 3 sc in last hdc; sc evenly across end of rows *(see Edging, page 24)*; working in free loops of beginning ch *(Fig. 56b, page 19)*, 3 sc in first ch, sc in next 38 chs, 3 sc in next ch; sc evenly across end of rows; join with slip st to first sc *(Figs. 27a & b, page 10)*, finish off *(Fig. 28, page 10)*.

We have made every effort to ensure that these instructions are accurate and complete. We cannot, however, be responsible for human error, typographical mistakes, or variations in individual work.

Projects made and instructions tested by Kathleen Hardy, Lisa Hightower, Tammy Kreimeyer, Ruth Landon, Ruby Lee, Faith Stewart, Clare Stringer, Carol Thompson, and Freida Ward.

ISBN 1-60140-210-4